" *Hyperlove* is a stylish and incisive lyric essay, dislocating the categories of love, desire, compulsion and control. Morris combines frank self-analysis and deft citation to create a tactile, woozy anatomy of the crush and its intimate politics. Hot, honest and irrational. **"**

Jack Underwood

" Simmering at the lovelorn altar with Simone Weil, Angel Olsen and Instagram, *Hyperlove* explores the 'Absolute Dirty Secret' of desire's imperative. With the assured grace of an essaying, diaristic lyric, Morris performs the swoon and sorrow of a radical longing. **"**

Maria Sledmere

" *Hyperlove* posits an assertively raw take on eros, walking the balance between control and frenzy. Naomi Morris' voice is lubricious, winking, and at times grimly comic. **"**

Alanna McArdle

HYPERLOVE

Edited by Robin Christian

Design and illustration by Patrick Fisher of Frontwards Design

Photograph by Robin Christian

 Available as an eBook and an audiobook with audio described cover and transcript.

ISBN: 978-1-8384362-2-3
eISBN: 978-1-8384362-5-4

First published in 2021 by Makina Books • makinabooks.com

Printed in the UK by Henry Ling Limited, at the Dorset Press, Dorchester

Makina Books: New Words Programme receives
financial assistance from the Arts Council of England

Supported using public funding by
ARTS COUNCIL ENGLAND

Naomi Morris

" ...in many individuals in whom separateness is not relieved in other ways, the search for the sexual orgasm assumes a function which makes it not very different from alcoholism and drug addiction. It becomes a desperate attempt to escape the anxiety engendered by separateness... **"**

Erich Fromm, *The Art of Loving*

PROLOGUE

In the art gallery,

I realise I am asking (begging) him

to give me a reason

to not have sex with him.

And I can't find any.

What reasons could he give?

I know you well.

I care about you.

We cohabitate.

You are not mysterious to me.

I know you better than you know yourself.

*I've seen you in monstrous moments.**

*I see me (now)

Now I see me

in a grotesque hall.

Abhorrent weight

of blank air.

Concrete colonial

building of motion sick

-ness. White white

white space and

the guy I am trying to

impress from

American wealth.

Get a grip but

if I don't succeed now,

the opposite is pandemic.

The opposite is strolling towards

the station after a lonely

KFC, loosed

from my solidity

IN GLƆSGOW

my crushes were waiting

like a pink room,

erect as a nipple.

By night I was fixated

on the texture

of the areola.

In London, I escape

to a return. Watching

the same lights flicker.

Alone, I walk

an upward hilt:

that wide expansive

slope that appeared

when romance wore

a silk dressing gown.

YOU SAW ME IN MONSTROUS MOMENTS

Conversations that

occupied several

train carriages

are now careening

empty

like ballooned sacks.

I'd text

come home

and you'd

come home.

Then words disappeared:

an imperceptible curtain

hung between us.

In perfect continual motion, I am split-

-ting at the seams, tearing

along the perforation

and it's not

ending

HOLY GHOST ZONE

Heading for
the Piccadilly Line

a drop of jealousy
blooms like mould

a hot sauce stain
on my sternum

in the space
thumbs press to prayer

menstruating gives
me a break

a *spotting* staining
white cotton knickers

blood map in
the shape of a cross

THE LOVE WITCH

lies on a pentagram and whispers "love me" with a desperation I understand.

I realise so much I'm talking about this man or this man and this is what they did, can we somehow together figure out exactly what they think of me?

The Love Witch is subjected to unwanted touch during a ritual.

What are their likes and dislikes of my body and face?

This – her body – is where her power and vulnerability are contained.

Did I say anything that repelled them? Do they replay it in their head? What do they replay in their head?

The Love Witch can't stop herself hurtling down the freeway toward total submersion in another.

I tell you all the things that replay in mine.

What Erich Fromm described as 'complete fusion'.

The "truth" is, it's the way I want to subsume my "self"
into another "body".

The Love Witch fixates on a man who is talking to
another woman.

Forget the dense responsibility of living like Canary
Wharf crushing my bones.

She wants him, she deserves him, she hexes him to
fall for her, to ignore other women.

'Assign magical qualities to others' is what SLAA
says.

The Love Witch drugs the man / fucks the man / lets
him die / buries him lovingly / makes a spell jar with
her piss and blood.

I attempt to assign magical qualities to myself.

When the man is dead she can love him more truly.

And the "truth" is, this was the first film to see me for
what I am.

The Love Witch marries another man (dreamscape) then stabs him with her ceremonial dagger.

Is this "love" process a process of death and resurrection?

Fromm says 'sexual desire can be stimulated by the anxiety of aloneness, by the wish to conquer or be conquered, by vanity, by the wish to hurt and even *to destroy*, as much as it can be stimulated by love.'

Every new man more perfect than the last.

Until they aren't.

Ext. street - night.

Standing outside

The Asylum, smoking

while they sing

LaNd Of HoPe AnD gLoRy

and staring at a round face

from Cornwall or some other

seaside county.

Not letting myself for a moment think

this is not okay.

Until I am naked as a rabbit.

Until the moon has eclipsed in my throat.

Until rainfall after the Sabat.

19

Int. bedroom - morning.

Unsending the words I sent to someone

I am trying to forget:

"I did it again."

That moment was/

is monstrous

(to me).

I see it.

HOW MANY TIMES

have my eyes unpeeled to this feeling in the morning?
A desire to be pliable, melded like burning iron, my
metal smooth like the flow of magma.

He said something like *rough sex during the
apocalypse*
and I want to curdle within his torso,
to tie him to the banisters,

call him a centrist scumbag and
blame my ever-deepening over-
drafts on him.

/

And I will be forgiven
like the leftie cherub I am. The sensual, in-the-dirt
earthen sign. Owner of a fattened tongue.

I am willing and capable – with rose-flavoured lube –
to forget the world is literally in flames for one night
– and every other.

For him to whip me one more time
– until the next.

For him to receive my greatest nudes
– forever.

12TH DECEMBER 2019

And I realise.

My feet have ached with desire. I dream

of stairwells in blocks of flats. Our thighs burn

with a fervour.

No one can break

my heart like England can.

ABSOLUTE DIRTY SECRET

like a crusted tissue stuffed up her sleeve.

It is not that she has *that much* sex but how much
she likes it.

She thinks.

It is a challenge to hear a sex love sex song and not
assign it to a person or experience. ♫ Damaged
goods ♫

Unless you, like her, occasionally struggle to emote.

♫ Sometimes I'm thinking that I love you

but I know it's only lust ♫

/

She has always wanted to have *that much* sex.

She thinks.

It's only now she acts it out that the audience asks,

Are you sure about that?

She was before she read SLAA's description of a love and sex addict [1].

Don't give it away so easily.

/

---

[1] become sexually involved with and/or emotionally attached to people without knowing them/confuse love with neediness, physical and sexual attraction, pity and/or the need to rescue or be rescued/fear intimacy and commitment, continually search for relationships and sexual contacts/sexualize stress, guilt, loneliness, anger, shame, fear and envy/use sex or emotional dependence as substitutes for nurturing, care, and support/immobilised or seriously distracted by romantic or sexual obsessions or fantasies/avoid responsibility by attaching to people who are emotionally unavailable/stay enslaved to emotional dependency, romantic intrigue, or compulsive sexual activities/assign magical qualities to others

She returns from a haze of googling 'Kiki' after
hearing the name in a Mac DeMarco song.

She scrolls through Kiki's Instagram.

She torture porns herself.

She counts how often she does this with hot, talented
couples.

When she imagines being with a man, she imagines
it in pictures.

It is a wholly visual experience.

The lack of it makes her shrivel.

/

YouTube recommends her all the TAURUS ♥ LOVE ♥ TAROT READING (WHAT YOU HAVE BEEN WAITING FOR!!!) videos in the world.

But only if it resonates.

A sense of fate is all she had been waiting for.

Somebody who would knock on her window while she lies there, watching the videos.

/

Sometimes, she can't bear a book that describes good, romantic sex.

She can't bear hearing about her friends' crushes going well, going beautifully.

Although she should be happy for them.

She can't bear it even if it's going chaotically.

She can't bear films or TV with beautiful people falling in love.

Not like she could when she was young.

When she was young, she would load up the DVD player with every romantic story she could get her hands on.

Even better if they hinted at sex.

/

Crushes have *generative possibilities* [2].

Her mistake is the prospective crush generating life, not art.

In the worst of it, only making up herself alive for a date.

On bad days, she wants to rip out every part out of her that wants to feel.

If she let herself – if she could bear it – she'd live in days as long and dark as a coffin.

2 Anne Boyer, 'The One and Only' in *Mal N° 1: That Obscure Object*, 2018.

IF SEX AND LOVE ADDICTION IS A THING, IT'S NOT GONNA KILL YOU [3]

How much is sex and love addiction, and how much is being a woman with OCD in the world?

How much is sex and love addiction, and how much is being a woman in the world?

How much is sex and love addiction, and how much is being a woman?

How much is sex and love addiction, and how much is being?

---

3 I decide to sell my Carly Rae Jepsen tickets because all her songs are about love. I walk through Peckham in the dark to pass them on in an envelope to a stranger, like dealing in pop songs. The next week, I see Angel Olsen with a close and important friend.

INTERMISSION

At the party:

I am raw

like a deer

just born

in a web

of sticky amniotics.

I feel my shadow

imprint on an unknown

house, bleached

out. Like tarmac

in a heatwave,

I am rippling

with envy.

Manic pixie dream girls fucked up a generation.

I always wanted to be the person that was wanted

the most, though couldn't want back in the same way

because they were in someway un-

-knowable. They would never open up and yet some-

-how exist as gorgeously vulnerable. Like,

fuck, I wish I had an exact and definable

trauma. I wish I had learnt how to avoid blowing

my own guts out

on the pavement.

On Tumblr, my username was
boycrazypatriarchyhater.

I've always been a crush-heavy character.

When I was 14, I had to run to my bedroom and cry
after seeing a boy's naked back on TV.

Last night I watched *Cave of Forgotten Dreams* and it
was the same feeling.

I was deep in a cavern of naked boy's backs.

Not to demean or cheapen the beginning of human
civilisation.

But to reveal my sensation of absolute terror meets
absolute beauty.

And the tenderness with which the archaeologists
stroked their knowledge into those rippled backs.

It also makes me want to vom.

In both instances, I was pre-menstruating.

I warp upon a jagged cliff of every

breakfast in the morning

I haven't been given.

(Everything is about me and

that's a really heavy burden.)

SPEAK IN TONGUES

My tongue, slug

in his (1) mouth.

My tongue, clefting

figure eights on him (2).

My tongue, subject

of texts he (3) shouldn't

be sending. My tongue,

compulsive as an earth

worm (4). My tongue,

tracing letters in the

soil. My tongue (5).

EKSTASIS
(OR: ANGEL OLSEN, MYSTIC)

'...ekstasis, *literally "standing outside oneself", a condition regarded by the Greeks as typical of mad persons, geniuses and* lovers...' (Anne Carson, *Decreation*)

The mystics were mad persons (women), geniuses, and lovers (of God).

Angel Olsen sings *give me some heaven / just for a while / make me eternal.*

There is a contradiction in her *while* vs. *eternal.*

An eternal ultimately equates to a nothingness.

Although nothing is something,

which is all we could want from God / Sex / Love.

It can be said that sex addiction is mistaking sex for God [4].

For the mystics [5], there was no partaking in Sex/God that centred the self. Their purpose was to lose the 'I' that we all endlessly strive to find, and then carelessly or painstakingly lose.

They willingly offered the self back over to a God who gave it to them in the first place. Sacrificing identity / *Absolute poverty* / Nothingness.

An obsession with sex or love or both (without God) allows one to temporarily be whoever one wants to be.

Or no one.

---

4 A claim made by Charlotte David Kasl in *Women, Sex, and Addiction: A Search for Love and Power*, Ticknor & Fields, 1989.

5 Anne Carson uses Sappho, Marguerite Porete, and Simone Weil as examples in *Decreation: Poetry, Essays, Opera*, Alfred A. Knopf, 2005. My favourite mystic, apart from Angel Olsen, is Julian of Norwich.

41

I remember pieces of the Old Testament from reading it as a child.

I remember that after Moses saw a glimpse of God, his face glowed from the brightness of it.

The whole sight of God, however, would be too much: *man shall not see me and live.*

Marguerite Porete describes the route to ecstasy in *The Mirror of Simple Souls.* The WILL and the SOUL depart from each other.

Which is essentially a little death.

A lightning bolt from heaven was enough to temporarily blind St. Paul.

The way my sight clouds if I stand up too quickly. If I orgasm too harshly while not lying down.

I often think that if anyone could look at the Sun close up without already being consumed by flames, they would burn up internally from the awe of it. A combustion of the soul.

Saint Theresa was visited by an angel whose *face was so aflame*, he seemed to be *all on fire*. Bernini immortalised this moment in his statue 'The Ecstasy of Saint Theresa'. Her expression is orgasmic.

When Sappho looks at her lover, *fire is racing under the skin / and in eyes no sight.*

Angel *goes blind*

every time.

All of which undermines the reality of physical blindness.

To use the phrase too liberally.

Of course, we do not *go blind*. But it is hard to resist this metaphor's easy access towards a loss of perception:

Does being metaphorically blind excuse us? Allow us to sin?

In the Bible, blindness was often a representation of being spiritually lost.

I see me through poetry. A momentary lapse in the desiring to be seen through the eyes of someone else.

Angel Olsen sings about the desire to be seen as if
she is owed it, that her ex/potential lover is "blind" to
not see HER (Maybe on purpose / Maybe the sight of
her would blind them).

If I'm out of sight then take another look around.

I act sticky in public when I think I am being looked at
/ when I expect to be looked at / when I am longing to
be looked at.

Walking around the same city as the person who
broke my heart, permanently fixed in a state of
expectation (they will see me / I won't see them).

Simultaneously fantasising about being picked out in
a crowd (as special / by a stranger).

At the art gallery, at the party, at the cafe, at the
Angel Olsen gig.

I bought a secondhand copy of *Why We Love* by Helen Fisher after a particularly nefarious heartbreak in my first year of university.

I wanted answers.

The first ingredient: "Repeat Exposure" showed that love was forged by the repetitive sight of the same person. To look, to see, to be exposed to, was apparently all it took.

Usually a mystic has more than one vision.

I also bought *The Ethical Slut* from Gay's the Word.

Eventually, I had many repetitive encounters with different people.

I asked myself if I was repeating this behaviour in the hope that I would eventually feel *the breath of God in my mouth* [6].

Or whether I was simply, a

"liberated woman".

---

6 A lyric from 'Seekers Who Are Lovers' by The Cocteau Twins. Elizabeth Fraser, arguably another musical mystic, often sings no discernable words, a kind of glossopoeia, or singing in tongues. Also in this song, the line *Jesus, God, Valentine*.

Many times I have tried to express how I am hyper-aware of every micro-movement around people I have a crush on, and, what if I have a crush on the whole world in that I want the whole world as a collective to fancy me, and, if the whole world fancies me than I can rest on that burden of proof that I am fanciable, and, when someone singular has a crush on me it's like 'oh, what took you so long' rather than 'oh, you are mistaken'.

This is not the male gaze. The whole world is in one person and a person is the whole world, but it's all mainly a reflection of you seeing you.

If only I knew how to disappear, writes Simone Weil, *there would be a perfect union of love between God and the earth I tread...*

If only I could see a landscape as it is when I am not there.

If only I could experience desire without being the object of it.

I am longing for something slightly past
objectification

on the road towards actualisation.

Why does my essence feel best represented by a

statuesque

nude

mirror

selfie?

I know that John Berger said that women watch themselves being looked at. *In Ways of Seeing* he says:

The surveyor of woman in herself is male: the surveyed female. Thus she turns herself into an object -- and most particularly an object of vision: a sight.

But why does 'every sexual expression' seem to 'raise the question of false consciousness'. Women accused of 'succumbing to "the pornification of society" and altering bodies to please men'. [7]

In the chapel where the 'Ecstasy of Saint Theresa' lives, there are chiselled theatre boxes on either side where marble men are positioned to look at Saint Theresa. They marvel permanently.

A panopticon where even her ekstasis is a public show. Her eyelids are shut. She cannot watch them watch her.

---

[7] Emily Witt, *Future Sex*, Farrar, Straus and Giroux, 2016.

Yet this is a highly valued expression of a woman's ecstasy and desire from the 17th century. Only acceptable because it is shrouded in a layer of holiness.

Marguerite Porete, who wants to disappear into God, still *calls her book a* Mirror... *speaks in erotic language, referring to God as "overflowing and abundant Lover"* [8].

Does she also want to watch herself being watched by God as she annihilates her soul? Would she take a selfie?

In Angel's *All Mirrors*, the mirrors are erasing. The mirrors are losing beauty. The image of her is disappearing.

And yet – she records this evaporation [9].

---

8 Anne Carson, *Decreation: Poetry, Essays, Opera,* Alfred A. Knopf, 2005.

9 It is impossible to stand outside of oneself. Someone else has to do it. An excretion or the abject stands outside of oneself. A self-portrait, when a woman does it, is an excretion of self. Chris Kraus's BODY of work, for example, is what Eileen Myles calls an '...entirely ghastly, cunty exegesis'.

I want to stare at my phlegm and see my reality like a crystal ball.

Not reflection, but immersion. An astral projection of pure truth.

I would snort pure truth if I could.

(Annihilation of the soul is a desire for absolute feeling. So absolute it becomes nothing)

I would have sex until I got the answer (I would never get).

At the end of *All Mirrors*, Angel Olsen has partially recovered her sight. She has exited her cell. She understands that maybe she has been asking too much:

What is it you think I need? / Maybe it's too hard to see

A suggestion that to KEEP our perception rather than lose it, is harder.

She asks for something simpler, more sentimental, less all-enveloping.

Why don't you say you're with me now / With all of your heart?

EPILOGUE

In the cafe:

We are reading poetry.

He had been horsing

me to exile

and I felt blood

red tomatoes seeping.

A darkened figure

who misunderstood my

frequent fire

for a crime of arson.

I put my name down

to read

and read PROLOGUE

in front of him

(but I didn't)

AFTERWORD

Do you ever experience a cave-like sadness for an experience that isn't your own?

How can someone feel so strongly for a fiction? For stories they have been told again and again but are just that - stories.

*

A crush doesn't feel good anymore, it feels like a violence.

The shame of the pit-blackness of the emotion.

In the pitness: a child. A child who is very lonely. A child who is keenly aware of what she lacks.

And then the pitness makes itself known on Saturday evenings, the sky in the window for company.

And the pitness feels more acute when the sky is clear and when the sunset is pin pricked by clouds of unfamiliar softness.

And the pitness cries out especially when it is hot and
sunny, keen for shade.

The pitness feels affronted by an external tragedy, it's
gauze whisked aside by the materiality of lives lost.
Young life lost.

A person who was a baby even to the pitness.

*

The interfaces of popular dating sites were purposely
made to be 'the clean, well-lighted place'. An appeal
to women. An appeal – I think – to the pitness.

*

Crushes as a precipice over which you are wanting to fall, despite yourself.

An actor and a musician leave we-want-to-fuck evidence all over Instagram then meet in Ireland at the tail-end of a pandemic, probably in order to fuck.

I am meeting my husband at the tail-end of a pandemic. At a perceived lull. People who fell in love during lockdown (romantic), people who broke up during lockdown (tragic), people who got conned during lockdown and out of that cut/deep crack arose a precipitous melody that sounded like chaos but was actually anxious attachment.

Kissless sex.

And also, people die. People still die.

*

Everything I write is fractious and in some way perverse because that is the time it was chosen for me to live in. I am a good writer. I am a good writer but am surrounded by people who get paid per word, paid for an Instagram caption, paid to write a Vogue piece about discovering old designer clothes (one of Boris Johnson's fractious children. Fractious as in, they are all over the place and there is a new one, born amid a pandemic. *Feel sorry for the mother,* they said, *she is alone and frightened.* I know of many mothers who are alone and frightened and where is their sympathy? Where are the material provisions that would ensure they have a quality of life that is at least sufficient, even if they will never try on their old designer clothes?)

*

I spend my time in a virtual world where there is
no sex. I forget what it is to kiss for the first time
(it is only 4 months, it feels like forever). I forget so
much what it is to touch someone that I worry it'll
feel wrong to do it. I can live without it, and that's
terrifying. I spend my time imagining what it would
be like to be a mystic. To give up so much and gain it
all. I want to wear a hazelnut around my neck. *It is all
that is made.*

How can I write in a way that fits into a category
pre-made (as in there when I was born)? Everything I
write is fractious and in some way perverse because,
when people write into a conformed structure, I feel
queasy. I don't know what FRONTAGE we are trying
to preserve. Doesn't a new way of the world mean a
new way of writing? Can we not have a break from
New York ------- op-eds from white people?

MORAL REDEMPTION 2021

I understand the need to submit to a consummation,
a way of not feeling every rivet of discomforting
emotion, a hyperlove.

Hyperlove smooths it all out and together by utilising
a single outlet (whether one person or many, the
chase produces a similar somatic reaction).

Hyperlove gives existentialism an easy vessel.
Creased, visceral, a target that is both you and the
other person (people) the same.

Hyperlove removes distinctions, fears the
unbridgeable gap between self and others and so
erases it entirely. Hyperlove subsumes to avoid
responsibility.

Hyperlove is an understandable reaction to the world
as is.

Braver still to submit to feeling everything without
another person to hold (or be!) the entrails. My love
sees the entrails with me.

My love is him but also friends, comrades, near
strangers whether through art or internet and me
again through all these people and pets and trees
and commutes and memories and paper and dinner
and lifting and pauses and crying and writing and
words.

My love is not hyper. It is strained and patient and
impatient and silent and miraculous and joyous and
forever and mortal and the world as it is but also
striving towards the world as it could be (forever).

*

She writes this. She Googles a hot, talented couple.

ACKNOWLEDGEMENTS

Thank you Robin for trusting *Hyperlove*. Thank you Kandace for looking at this in all its raw states and always having something to say about it. Thank you Daisy for everything, always. Thank you Edith Fan Club. Thank you Eleri for all the *Mums on Tour*. Thank you Hannah, Cat and Suzie for being the best housemates. Thank you Eloise for the clarifying attachment walks. Thank you family for hopefully not reading this. Thank you to all my past teachers, especially Jack. Thank you to everyone on my Instagram 'Close Friends'. Thank you Joe for reading this on one of our first dates.